I0476390

The Market Leader Formula

'A Proven 3 Step System For Creating a Consistent Stream of Customers and a Stable Thriving Business In Less Than 14 Minutes Per Day'

By Patrick Dahdal

Legal Notice

While all attempts have been made to verify the information provided within this publication, neither the Author nor the Publisher assume any responsibility for any errors, omissions, or contrary interpretations of the subject matter herein.

This publication is not intended for use as a source of legal or accounting advice. The Publisher wants to stress that the information contained herein may be subject to varying states and/or local laws or regulations. All users are advised to request competent counseling in order to determine what state and/or local laws or regulations may apply to their particular business.

The Purchaser or Reader of this publication assumes full responsibility for the use of these materials and information. Adherence to all applicable federal, state, and local laws and regulations, as well as the ones governing professional licensing, business practices, advertising, and any other aspects regarding the prosecution of doing business in the United States or any other jurisdiction is the sole responsibility of the Purchaser or Reader.

The Author and Publisher assume no responsibility or liability whatsoever on behalf of any Purchaser or Reader of these materials.

Any perceived resemblance to specific people or organizations is unintentional.

Table of Contents

It's harder today which is why you have to be smarter

As a small business owner today we are experiencing a much more difficult climate in where we can grow our business, make a decent living and have certainty that our business will be profitable in future. What has made it harder for us is the increasing costs of advertising and more businesses competing to get our prospective customers. There is also the stress to keep up with technology and consistently learn new online marketing tactics. In addition to all this consumers are being more immune to our marketing messages. The trust in society is at an all-time low and consumers don't know who they can trust to help them solve their problems, frustrations or desires.

Here is some interesting statistics from Constant Contact:

- 59% of small business owners say it's harder to run a small business now than it was just five years ago.
- 55% of business think it's the economy.
- 49% of business think it's keeping up with technology (online marketing)
- 40% of business think it's to competition.

Another interesting statistic from Constant Contact is this one which shows the top concerns of small business owners:

Here are the top concerns 5 years ago:
- 78% think getting new customers is a top concern
- 61% think they are low on time is a top concern
- 49% think keeping customers is a top concern

Here are the top concerns today:
- 75% think getting new customers is a top concern
- 65% think they are low on time is a top concern
- 58% think keeping customers is a top concern

What is interesting here is that we can see that keeping customers has had the biggest increase with a 9% increase as a concern, this shows that competition is fiercer than even 5 years ago.

Another interesting statistic shows that nearly half of small business owners have a difficult time keeping with technology and what to focus on when it comes to online marketing, and it's fully understandable as the online marketing space is changing rapidly and what worked yesterday is not as effective anymore.

With the increase of competition and a rapidly changing online marketing environment as well as traditional marketing not being as effective anymore and some even say that traditional marketing is dead, what do you do?

Before I answer that, here is what Harvard Business Review has to say about traditional marketing:

*"...buyers are no longer paying much attention. Several studies have confirmed that in the "buyer's decision journey," traditional marketing communications just aren't relevant. Buyers are checking out product and service information in their own way, often through the Internet, and often from sources outside the firm such as **word-of-mouth or customer reviews.**"*

Which is understandable since majority of consumers have a low trust factor when it comes to advertisements and marketing, here is what Marketing Week has to say about that:

*"The **majority of UK consumers don't trust** what companies say in their advertising"*

This is not just applicable to the UK this tendency is well spread all over the western world.

With all this in mind, what can you do?

Decide to shift from the traditional marketing avenues and the traditional online marketing methods and embrace what we I call 'The Market Leader Formula'.

In this book I will show you why being a market leader, and specifically my three step market leader formula, is your best vehicle to attract quality customers, generate more sales consistently and have thriving business no matter the economic situation. You will discover what the market leader formula is and how you can implement it in your business without spending more money on advertising, flyer drops, social media advertising or SEO strategies on your website, and how to set it all up so it requires less than 14 minutes per day.

Now is the right time to embrace the opportunity to become a market leader as 95% of small business owners haven't taken any action or leveraged this effective and proven marketing model. My prediction is that for the next 18-24 months you have an open field to put your sticks in the ground, dominate your industry and become the market leader which in turn will profit proof your business for years to come.

What is 'The Market Leader Formula'?

The market leader formula is an effective marketing strategy comprised of three specific marketing activities that positions you as the market leader. We will go through them here.

But first…

Why is it important be the market leader?

Because your prospective customers, clients or patients want the market leader. They want the market leader as for them seeing all the choices of different businesses offering the same services is confusing. They don't know who to trust, who is going to care of them and who is going to give them the results that they want. In order for them to know who they can trust, they are going to go to the business they think is the market leader and this is the business that has made a conscious marketing effort in positioning themselves as the market leader.

This is even more important if you're a local business serving a particular geographical area as consumers today in the local space wants to build a relationship with you, they want to know you have their best interest in mind and for them the way to discover that is to have a conversation with you, come into your business and have a raving fan experience i.e. they love how they have been treated and the results they got from interacting with you that they want to spread it to the world.

Consumers today are fed up with the faceless corporations and want a personable business that can become their trusted advisor in matters that concerns what you're offering, they want the personal touch and they want to be educated so they can make the best possible decision of which service is best going to suit them. If you're the one who is doing the educating you will be the one who is considered the expert, the market leader and they will come to you, they will become your customer.

How do you become the market leader?

Great question.

This is where we will start to dive into 'The Market Leader Formula'. There are three steps to the market leader formula and each step build on each other. They strengthen each other and when you put all the three steps into action in your business you will be the market leader.

Step 1: Develop Your 5 Star Reputation & Market That Reputation to Get More Customers

Having a 5 star reputation is really the foundation for any other marketing you're doing. A study done by Bright Local in 2014 showed that **85% of consumers read up to 10 reviews in order for them to trust a business.** This trend will continue and become more important as consumers are used to seeing a lot of reviews when choosing to buy products or services. Just look at Amazon, Ebay or Trip advisor each product or destination have reviews in the hundreds. This means consumers expect to see many high rated reviews in order to trust a business and contact them in the first place.

Here is another interesting statistic (Bright Local):

88% of consumers say they trust online reviews as much as personal recommendations.

This is important for you know as the more online 5 star reviews you have the more 'personal recommendations' you have online, working for your 24/7 generating new prospective customers to your doorstep.

We will go deeper into this in the chapter covering Step 1: Develop Your 5 Star Reputation & Market That Reputation to Get More Customers.

For now I want to leave you with two thoughts to think about when it comes to your reputation:

1. Your reputation is the foundation for all your other marketing activities. From my experience doing other marketing activities but not having your 5 star reputation in place will minimise your ROI on your other marketing

campaigns. If you have one bad review online and then run an online ad campaign, people will see your ad and then do their research about you online (which statistically 87% will do whether it's through an ad or word of mouth) to find out more about your company and then finds the one bad review. You have now lost not only that potential customer but you will have also lost money on that ad.

2. Your reputation only starts with what in the industry is called reputation management as monitoring your reviews online and handling any bad reviews doesn't directly generate income for you. Managing doesn't make you money, marketing does. This is why you want to do what we call 'Reputation Marketing' which includes as one element reputation management but there are two other elements maybe even more important which I'll share with you in the chapter on reputation later in this book.

Let's get into Step 2…

Step 2: Create High Quality Videos Educating Your Prospective Customers and Market These Videos on All Major Online Platforms

Again here we are meeting the trends set by consumer behaviour as well as Google and YouTube.

If you're not engaged in video and video marketing you are losing out on business. Here is what The Guardian had to say in an article in July 2014:

"With online video quickly becoming a key means for people to satisfy their information and entertainment needs, <u>small businesses that fail to include it in their internet marketing strategies will do so at their peril.</u>"

This is why you need to seriously consider adding video marketing into your arsenal of marketing activities, and it's going to be more important than ever if you want to future proof your business.

Why?

See here what Cisco is predicting when it comes to video:

"By 2017 video will account for 69% of all consumer traffic on the internet"

This is presents a huge opportunity as most local businesses haven't leveraged video marketing the right way and hence for most markets and geographical areas you have an opportunity to start your video content marketing strategy and dominate your industry and area by using video.

The businesses that capitalises on this now in 2015 and 2016 will have an unbeatable advantage over those who don't, and guess who will be considered the market leader and get the customers.

When you develop your video content you want to develop it to educate your prospective customers and answer their most frequently asked questions as well as educate them on different aspects of your products and services. You want to give them tips on what to look for when making a decision on that particular service or product you are offering. By creating video content this way you are doing the following which will get your more customers and become the market leader:

1. **You are educating** – the videos will be engaging your audience by providing interesting video content that teaches them more about your products, services and brand.

2. **You are entertaining** – you are connecting with your audience by using your personality, they get to see you and get to know you, and thus get to like you.

3. **You are promoting** – as you are creating value added videos that gives your audience content that matters to them in the moment when they are conducting research to solve their problems, frustrations and/or desires that your products and services solve, you are essentially positioning yourself as the solution.

This is the most effective way to promote yourself as you are not 'pitching' or 'selling' your services or products but instead educating them by answering questions they already have. Consumers are tired of sales messages bombarding them every day in every way (TV, newspapers, flyers in the mailbox, internet and radio etc.), they have gotten immune to it and I'm sure the same goes for you. If you're like most small business owners how many calls or emails do you get every day with sales and marketing messages?

The way to stand out is to lead with value and give value to your customers before asking for anything. This is what you're doing when you're creating video content the right way. You're positioning yourself as the expert, the market leader.

If you're not convinced yet here are further research data showing you why video is important:

- **96% of consumers** surveyed found videos helpful for making online purchase decisions
- **71% of consumers** surveyed confirmed watching a video left them with a positive impression of the brand, service or company
- **73% of all consumers** are more likely to make a purchase after watching videos explaining a product or service
  (source: animoto)

We will go deeper into this in the chapter on video content marketing and I'll give you some steps you can take to start claiming your expert positioning, become the marker leader and future proof your business.

Step 3: Create a Marketing Funnel That Engages and Converts Prospective Customers to Your Customer

One of the most important marketing elements for your business is having a marketing funnel, this is also the most misunderstood and in majority of cases never implemented.

What is a marketing funnel?

A marketing funnel is a process whereby you take a prospective customer and by them going through your marketing funnel will end up as a customer for one or several of your services or products.

Why do you want a marketing funnel?

Most businesses idea of marketing is what I call random acts of marketing activities. In majority of cases they use a marketing tactic not based on an overall strategy but instead with the objective of only trying to get a customer which I'll explain below is a flawed way and more expensive way of doing marketing. In many cases it is just advertising what services you provide and sometimes a special offer.

However this kind of marketing is not as effective anymore (as shown in the research data beginning of the book) and it also caters to a small percentage of your market place: mainly the person who in that moment in time see your ad or flyer and they need your service right then and there. Typically this accounts for only 3% of the market place at any given time.

This means that this type of marketing doesn't cater to the other 97% who isn't in need of your services or products right now, they might be in a week from now or a month from now or three months from now but because your ad only caters to the person who needs it right now you're losing potential customers and are missing out on maximising your marketing money.

This is where a marketing funnel constructed the right way will not only convert more of the people who need your services or products right now but will also convert the people who might need them in a week from now or month from now or six months from now; and because you caught these people ahead of time they will now be your customer as your marketing funnel has got them into your sphere of influence and now you can educate them through your marketing funnel and the videos you've created.

To further illustrate the importance of creating a marketing funnel here is what I call 'The Consumer Pyramid':

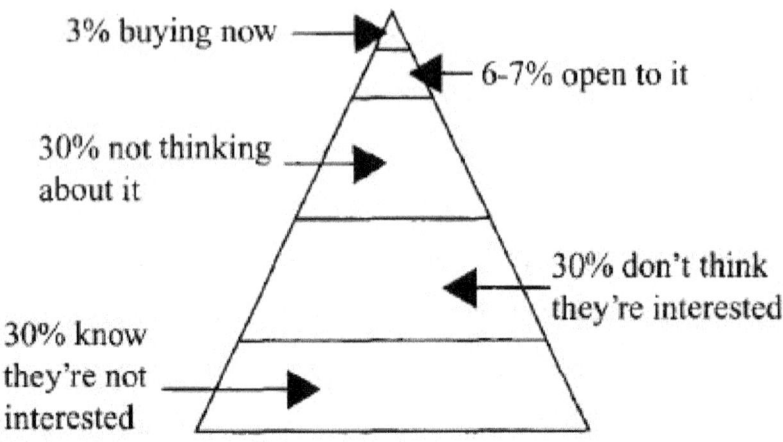

(The research done for the consumer pyramid was done by Chet Holmes a brilliant marketer and business growth expert who unfortunately passed away but this wisdom is still with us)

To set the scene for the consumer pyramid, imagine you got the opportunity to stand in a stadium filled with over hundred thousand people from your local area and you got the opportunity to talk about your business and what you're offering. Research has shown that only 3% of people in that stadium would be interested in your service right then and there, right in that moment. If we asked the people in that stadium the question: 'How many of you are in the market right now for a dentist?' we would get around 3 %. If we asked same about furniture, cars or a chiropractor etc., we would get the same percentage or close to it. About 3% of potential buyers in any given moment are buying now.

Then we have 7% who are open to it. These are potential customers who are not happy with their current provider or are thinking about looking for a new provider that can serve them better. These are people who are open to buying what you provide, maybe not right now but in the near future.

Then we have the remaining 90%.

The first set of 30% on the pyramid are not thinking about it, that is they are not against it or they are not actively looking for your services, they are just not thinking about it. This means that if you had a marketing campaign going 30% of the people seeing it are not thinking about what you're offering.

The second set of 30% on the pyramid don't think they're interested. They are not neutral like the first set of 30% above, these people might email you and say they are not interested if you did an email campaign to them because they don't know they are interested.

The last set of 30% on the pyramid know they're not interested because they are happy with what they have now. They have a car that has been working well for five years so in their mind there is no reason to change.

Now let's get you back in that stadium and you still have the opportunity to talk about your offer. However before you are given the mic to speak the host says to everyone in the audience "If what this person is going to talk to you about today is of no interest to you simply feel free to leave".

Now it's your turn to speak and you say (assuming you're a dentist of course): "My dental services are top notch, we use the latest technologies and have a rigorous continual education to keep on top of the latest techniques to give you a confident smile that you'll be proud of". Unfortunately 90-97% of the audience will walk out, and if you ever been speaking in front of people you know you don't want that.

With this in mind.

What could you say that would have virtually everyone stay in their seats to listen to you? This is a question you want ask and answer because this is what's going catapult your revenue, profits and make you the market leader. The marketing message you develop from this question is the same message you want to use for your website and for all those potential buyers in the stadium to keep them in their 'seats'.

This is why a carefully crafted marketing funnel done the right way is important for your business growth, business profit and business future. It's not uncommon by implementing a marketing funnel the way I'm going to show you in this book that a business can increase their sales by 100 to 300%. I know this might sound too good to be true however hang in there and I'll show you how this happens.

This is the first version of this book and in it you will find how to implement Step 3 in your business i.e. 'The Marketing Funnel'. The other two steps you can access by going to my website http://www.marketleaderformula.com as those two steps are best learned by visuals, this is why you got free access to my webinar covering the first two steps, which are 'Reputation Marketing' and 'Video Content Marketing'.

The other reason I chose to go through the marketing funnel in the book is because implementing this step first will give you the quickest ROI on your time and money. This is the fastest way to leverage the marketing you are already doing today.

If you want to get in touch or are interested in getting our assistance to implement these steps in your business please visit my website:

http://www.marketleaderformula.com

To your success,
Patrick Dahdal

The Marketing Funnel Blueprint

The Internet marketing business had evolved throughout the years. If you have been in this business long enough, you have probably witnessed the numerous changes occurred in the past decade. At its birth, the Internet marketer only offered one product to customers.

Nowadays, we have a marketing funnel.

Changes have come about so quickly that everything has been shaped to fulfill the needs of buyers. Due to the evolution of the Internet that has been taking place over the past decades, the scope has grown to an epic proportion. With larger and larger audiences, things are bound to change. Internet business-making has kept up to the fast pace of changes and adapted to its demands.

The Marketing Funnel Blueprint is the latest strategy that new businesses don't know about yet. If you're not using this strategy in your business you are most likely leaving big opportunities on the table.

In this book, I will uncover all of the secret techniques other businesses use to achieve a twofold or threefold increase in their revenues. Just by applying the Marketing Funnel to your business, you will get immediate results without worrying about marketing your products.

Now, let's get down to business.

Why should you use the Marketing Funnel?

As previously mentioned, Internet marketing has evolved from selling only one product to the present model, which I am going to further explain throughout the book. The first reason why businesses need the Marketing Funnel is basically because putting all your eggs in one basket isn't enough anymore; you can't rely on just one product. Besides, we all want to keep moving ahead, don't we?

In former years, businesses would only sell one product at a higher price and still earned enough money. Nonetheless, the competitiveness of Internet businesses is getting tougher and tougher as time goes by. Thus, the marketing model has ripened to what we have today, adding more products and assembling what is now known as the Marketing Funnel.

Most importantly, this is a guaranteed technique to increase your revenues. Not requiring any additional work, traffic or effort, you can increase your income, as simple as that. All you need to do is focus on redirecting Internet traffic to your site, getting people to purchase your front-end product, and the Marketing Funnel will do the rest.

As always, all the normal groundwork will still be your duty, which consists in sending promotional emails to your subscribers and recruiting JVs and affiliates. There's just one additional phase here, which is the marketing funnel. Establish the Marketing Funnel in the marketplace, and have it operate at full length during your sales campaign. The best part is that you can make it fly solo automatically.

There's just one tiny difference compared to the previous method, though: you will get twice or three times as much income, almost immediately.

You'll be able to see the results within 48 hours of implementing this technique.

The Marketing Funnel Formula

Upon learning how advantageous applying the Marketing Funnel in your business will turn out to be, it is time to understand the Marketing Funnel concept. Here is the formula:

As exhibited in the chart, the Marketing Funnel starts with:

1. Front-end,
2. Profit Maximizer 1,
3. Downsell,
4. Profit Maximizer 2,
5. Profit Maximizer 3, and
6. Back-end.

It's really a lot more complex than that, but we'll explain it better as we unveil each topic, one-by-one.

You will hear a lot of novel terms in The Marketing Funnel, so let me introduce the terms before we study them separately in the latter chapters. First of all, the frontline product is called a **front-end** product. Front-end products are paramount in comparison to others.

Even though its selling price is lower than the others, if you don't open the 'buying loop' via the front-end product, the whole Marketing Funnel won't do its job. It's like a gateway into a whole different world that the marketing funnel is.

Following this, we have the Profit Maximizer. If you notice the chart previously shown, the Profit Maximizer takes place 3 times during the whole marketing funnel. If front-end products serve as the entry for the buying loop, then the Profit Maximizers are the principal origin of your revenues.

The Profit Maximizer is an immediate offer after your front-end product or a product that suits the particular needs or problems of customers. These needs or solutions for clients are usually placed in either Profit Maximizer 2 or Profit Maximizer 3, because the price elevates as we go through each tier.

The price increases from Profit Maximizer 1 to Profit Maximizer 3. The price of your front-end sets the prices for the other products in the marketing funnel. This will be clarified later.

And then, the element after the Profit Maximizer 1 is called the **down-sell**. Down-sell is the lower price version of the Profit Maximizer 1. It happens right after Profit Maximizer 1. The down-sell is nothing more than the same product with a diminished price.

Some of the buyers may think that Profit Maximizer 1 isn't worth it. Therefore, the down-sell was established.

The final product down the funnel is a **Back-end**. Usually the Back-end offer is presented to customers with the follow-up emails after a few days. A Back-end could be in the format of a webinar, some coaching, a coaching group, and many more. Normally, the Back-end product is the product with the highest price in contrast to the other items in the marketing funnel.

As specified before, a Back-end offer is made after a few days in your follow-up emails to your clients. Why? Because you'll need a few days to build up a good reputation through the other products they purchased from you and your follow-up emails. You have to make them trust you before you offer them the Back-end; this is the key to sealing a Back-end offer deal.

In this book, I will show you the steps so that you can create and constitute your own marketing funnel. I can guarantee you the instant result of increasing in your incomes within 48 hours, just by employing the marketing funnel.

Patrick Dahdal

How to Create an Irresistible Front-End Offer

As you already know, front-end products will be your frontline products. It is important to make your front-end irresistible. The front-end offer has the most significant role among others in the marketing funnel, because it is going to allure people and set things in motion with the marketing funnel.

Lacking an irresistible front-end offer to open the loop, it doesn't matter how fantastic your Profit Maximizer offer may be, or how great your Back-end offer is, people will not notice them. So, it is of the utmost importance to ensure they get your front-end offer.

You'll learn some key concepts regarding front-end products aw you walk you way in this chapter, but counting on an irresistible front-end offer is the foundation to a successful online business. When the front-end offer makes the first sales, you can multiply them by channeling them through the marketing funnel.

Your front-end product is the first one you'll show to subscribers. Essentially, it gives the first impression of your Marketing Funnel to the people that click into your sales website. That's why a seductive front-end product is so important to keep things running through its course.

Although a bad front-end could spoil the whole funnel, a great front-end could attract your subscribers to buy all over your marketing funnel. A front-end product is normally sold at a low price. Its principal aim is to attract subscribers to click on the "Buy" button. In fact, a product launching is really intense. As the launch itself is happening, you must be there monitoring everything to make changes. Most of the times, price-related issues are common factors that lead to a low selling rate.

That's why I strongly recommend you to keep track of the price of your front-end product during the exhibition of your products in your marketing funnel. It is a time-tested price range for the front-end, that could start at $9.97 and go up to $37 and so on. Be that as it may, there are no fix or unbreakable rules here; you can always adjust the price accordingly.

Now, you may think that setting your front-end product at a low price couldn't generate huge profit, even if you sell a thousand products or more. With a 100% commission given out to the affiliate, where does the profit come from? Let me tell you something: don't worry about this. Real money doesn't come from your front-end. **It comes from your Profit Maximizers and Back-ends.**

I hope you now understand the whole concept of the marketing funnel. The front-end can hardly give you any profit, because you will offer your affiliate a 100% commission. The front-end only functions as the opening key of the buying loop. This is why you need the marketing funnel.

Criteria of Front-End

To create a front-end offer that is irresistible, you must first create a product that has a mass appeal, which could generate huge amounts of sales. Before choosing the theme and purpose of your front-end, do some marketing research. First, understand what kind of market you are going to cover, and then investigate the customers that actually dwell in the niche.

Researching is crucial, because in different types of niche, you'll find different kinds of customers with different mindsets. If you can think in the same way your ideal customers would, attract some traffic to your site and generate big sales, you're not that far.

First of all, target a larger market like an Internet marketing niche or a personal development niche. Both options are likely to generate an important amount of sales. Identify the market and the front-end product that you can sell in it. When you can finally target the people in it, your front-end offer is going to make massive sales by itself.

The second aspect to consider of a front-end product is, of course, an evergreen topic. An evergreen topic is a topic that will attract more people to buy and will last a very long time. People will still need the product, regardless of what kind of business they are in.

For example, lead generation methods would be an evergreen topic in the Internet marketing niche. Independently of what kind of Internet businesses they are in, they will definitely need to get visitors and subscribers to their website. This is a topic that will never grow old, especially for email marketing as a whole. A product vendor will need it, and so will an affiliate; as long as it involves email marketing, they will need your product to make their list grow.

For this session, in order to decide what kind of topics are evergreen topics, you'll need to analyze your ideal customers too. Don't hesitate to invest your time performing some research on your customers' preferences, because this will definitely help in your marketing funnel, both short-term and, more importantly, long-term. I will not teach you much on how to conduct some research in this book, because it is a whole different topic that would deviate us from the marketing funnel.

The third criterion of a front-end offer is a feature that can solve an immediate or urgent problem. Think about it, why do people want to buy your product? It's because they need a quick solution to solve a problem. If your product can solve their problem immediately, it is what people are looking for.

When you offer a solution to their problems, you are in fact implementing the skill of emotionally enhancing your products.

Emotional enhancers include:

Wealth/Money	Happiness
Security	Health
Power	Recognition
Love	

Of course, there are many more besides these. The ones listed here are the most effective emotional enhancers that you could make use of. When you are brainstorming for ideas, always remember how to apply these to your products.

What you can do before you set the topic for your front-end is to ask yourself a few questions:

- How can I enhance this product and make it irresistible?
- How can I push the 'emotional buttons' that everyone has?
- How do emotional enhancers apply to this product?

Always consider that you can incorporate and entwine several emotional enhancers. You don't have to use only one at a time. To make it easier for you, I have already prepared a checklist for you. When you are brainstorming ideas for your product, follow the checklist. Write down every single idea that comes to your mind and cross them out only after a long and thoughtful consideration.

Format of Front-End

Your front-end product could take various forms, such as an e-book, a series of videos with a compilation of transcripts, some graphics, etc. If you are familiar with the digital products marketplace, you know these are the 3 common formats that have been used for years. As I mentioned earlier, understanding your target market is really important.

If you manage to figure your target market out, you'll gain a deep insight on their preference. For example, for the Internet marketing niche, people in that market couldn't invest too much time reading. The mutable ambiance and platforms in the Internet marketing niche don't allow them to spare their time.

Accordingly, most of them prefer to have videos and transcripts instead of a book. Once again, this is not a 'must'; you can offer e-book as your front-end as well.

Writing an e-book is more convenient for you compared than publishing a physical book. You can avoid the tiring logistic work of publishing the book, while preserving your budget to be used in other important tasks (not to mention, trees will love you for it!). All you have to do is just write the content and upload the file. That's all there is to it. Evidently, you can see how convenient it is to write an e-book.

Moreover, here's a tip for you. After some time of publishing e-books, you can re-purpose the e-book by turning it into a physical book and selling it at a higher price. You may have to go through all the labor that you were spared of by writing an e-book instead, but consider the e-book platform as a starting point; we choose it because it's easier and we can also publish physical books later on.

You can compile the related e-books of yours that you created a long time ago, tweak the content a bit, and resell it at a higher price.

The sole drawback is that you have to deal with the logistic work, such as printing it out and sending it to the customers' doorstep. Investing your time to do this is definitely worth it, though. A physical book that is delivered to the doorstep of your house is more exclusive than the e-book that you can download anytime in the marketplace.

Some of the serious buyers may want to have a hard copy of your product, because it is easier and more accessible (in some ways). You can do this every now and then, to assess the conversion rate of selling a physical book as well. If selling physical book does work, you can consider offering it as one of your Profit Maximizers.

Besides the book format, you can turn it into a video training course including the compilation of transcripts. This is believed to be the most common format in the marketplace in present times. As I said before, although some people can study and learn better through reading, others learn better by watching and listening.

Additionally, to be frank, people who love reading are becoming fewer in recent years. A part of this is due to their busy daily schedule or because of work as well. Not many people can squeeze some extra time to read a 100-page book, but they wouldn't mind listening to it.

This is a reason amid several why audiobooks are 'in' right now. People simply don't have enough time anymore, or perhaps, they're getting more and more impatient; thus, the short attention span.

If you can turn 100 pages' worth of content into a 20 to 30 minutes course, why not? They can at least listen to the content of the training course, and if they miss anything out, they could look at the transcript.

Occasionally, e-books can be sold paired with the videos and transcripts. You can offer both at the same time and set your price a little bit higher. If you're worried about the price being too high selling both in this way, you can re-purpose the e-book and turn it into a free report for your subscribers.

Mind this: a free report is usually a shorter version and a more general version of the actual e-book. For example, if your e-book is about generating traffic through different methods, you can change the title of the free report to *"How To Get Instant Traffic Through Buying Solo Ad"*. You are revealing the first method as a teaser for them to grasp the concept of traffic generation.

If they are serious about their business, they will buy your front-end to learn more about it. These are the ideal customers you should focus on; instead of only adding names to your 'subscribers list', you could increase your 'buyers list' too.

Graphics is another niche that is a huge market. Whoever owns a website will need graphics; whoever needs to give presentations, needs graphics as well. This is a potentially sizable market that you can try at first.

There are few front-end products that you can start with:

- PowerPoint or Keynotes templates,
- Infographics,

- Mascot creator

The list can grow larger, but these are just a few common graphic front-ends that you could find in the marketplace.

Methods to Get Front-End

So, this is how you can build up your front-end product. There are two ways you can get the front-end product:
- Create it by yourself, and
- Re-purpose PLR products.

The front-end product could take 3 formats as you already know, but don't hesitate; I will lead you step-by-step during the process of creating an irresistible front-end product in all of them.

Method #1: Create it yourself

E-book: First step, brainstorm for ideas. I hope you are aware of the importance of picking the right topic for your front-end product by now, because if the front-end can't manage to make the first sale and open the buying loop, the whole Marketing Funnel will be useless.

A great front-end offer allures people and sets thing on motion. Hence, brainstorming for ideas for your front-end product is essential. It is vital to understand your intention is to be able to create the product. For newcomers, once you've decided your target market, go out and make connections with the people that are already in it.

When you are doing this, first of all, you are widening your connection to the potential Joint Venture partners that you could associate with and work in the future. Furthermore, you are building up your credibility in this market. Heightening your credibility within the market is important, both for the business and visitors.

When you have built up certain credentials in the circle of business, people will promote your products willingly. Additionally, when you have boosted your credibility among visitors, your products will sell a lot more.

Enhancing your credibility is enhancing your brand. You don't have to be a scientist to know how important branding is. Branding plays a major role in sales and, in some instances, it does the actual selling for you, not the product's quality.

This is why improving your connection is so important too.

Another objective of establishing connections is for you to understand more about the kind of topics other businesses normally use. This will definitely help you through your brainstorming session.

For those who have been in the business long enough, brainstorming for ideas surely won't be that hard anymore. However, you must always be inventive. Comprehend the needs of your subscribers, and design a product that fulfills their needs. This is not a simple mission, but in order to survive this ever-changing industry, you must always be innovative. Either you make it or you're through.

Now, going back, after deciding what you are going to use for your front-end, you need to ask yourself a question: "How are you going to teach them?" This is the next problem to solve.

- Is it going to be from your own experience?
- Is it going to be from what you've learned by doing research?

If both ways are not applicable, evaluate and ponder on it once again until you get something that works.

Collect only indispensable materials for your content. Remember to focus exclusively on what you are going to teach. Most people tend to forget the first intention of creating the product. As a deduction, the information of the product isn't in-depth. If you follow the tips I've mentioned just now, you may have some idea on where to get the materials for your content by now.

Basically, you can write everything from the beginning based on your own experience and knowledge, or you can do your research online.

The most important step before you start writing is drafting your content. You can start first without a sequence. The order in which you present this sequence can always be modified afterwards. List down the chapters one-by-one, and then, put organize them to have the general overview of your e-book.

The next step would be to outline the sub-points that you are going to write in each chapter. Elaborating a basic draft of the chapters will ensure a smooth flow of the whole content.

Then, you can start writing the content. Writing an e-book isn't as easy as you may think. It will take more time to complete compared to creating the video training courses. You will need a proper structure, planning, and a lot of revision. It will take a very long time.

Sometimes, you may be experiencing writer's block in the midst of writing, but don't force yourself to keep writing. Take a short break, read an article that is unrelated to what you are writing, take a short nap, drink a cup of coffee. Refresh your mind and then continue your work.

The final step is discretionary. This is a step especially for rookies in the business. Get some feedbacks from others and then revise your product based on the feedbacks. Even if you are already familiar with the business, you may not want to skip this step. You can never produce something that is 100% perfect, so external feedbacks are still valuable.

If you're new to this world and still aren't sure about whether what you're doing is right or wrong, I strongly recommend you to get some PLR products as references reference your product.

Videos + Transcripts: The procedures to create a video training course and transcripts are quite similar to the ones to create an e-book, i.e., brainstorm for ideas first, collect the necessary materials for the content and then draft your content.

The first 3 steps are crucial because they will determine whether your front-end offer can generate massive sales or not. It will be slightly different when you're creating the content for the book and videos.

The initial step of creating the video is preparing some presentation slides using PowerPoint or Keynote for each module. There's a specific way to create the presentation slides as well.

First, change the visual format of you slides to an HD ratio (16:9). Traditional presentation slides used had the 4:3 layout, which is squarer in form. Today, the vast majority of computer screens are widescreen, so when you set them to a 16:9 ratio, your slides will have a better appearance at the moment of being displayed on full screen.

If you stick to the 4:3 layout, the sides will look empty when a video I shown on full screen in any widescreen computer. So, remember to change the layout to 16:9 before you start writing your points. Moreover, it will look more cinematic.

Another word of advice, don't fill 100% of your slides with words. The maximum you should think of is 80%, otherwise you'll lose people's attention due to the hefty content. Besides, the words will be overlap with the control panel of the players at the bottom of your slides.

The last criterion to bear in mind is summing up the important points in the slides, while other explanations will be presented in your transcripts. It's all right to have maybe just 2 or 3 points per slide; the rest could be thoroughly explained in you transcripts and let them listen to it later.

These are the things you should be careful about when creating your presentation slides. After taking care of that, the next thing you need to do is to write a transcript for each module.

The transcript has basically 2 aims: (1) Write the voice-over actor's speech, and (2) compile it along the video training course.

Once these 2 tasks are fulfilled (after the voice actor does the recording and the video is completed) your front-end offer is ready.

Graphics: Creating a graphic front-end offer is totally different from the last two formats recently mentioned. First, you'll need to hire a graphic designer to design the graphics for you.

Likewise, you'll have to come up with several ideas to create presentation slides, infographics, mascots or a higher end product like graphic software. You can skip the steps to collect materials for content and draft it yourself, except for infographic products.

When you are dealing with an infographic product, the content for the product is needed anyways. So, you will need somebody to write the content along with the graphic designer to make the infographics.

Method #2: Buy PLR Products

This is the most expedite way to create your front-end. With this method, you can even create a few front-end ahead and line up the launches for months. This technique will save you so much time that you'll be able to look out for important businesses.

It doesn't matter if you are writing an e-book or a video training course, what you need to do is gather a few PLR products that are related and rewrite it. The best characteristic of a PLR product is that you are allowed to resell the products without any copyright issues.

How to Make Your Offer Irresistible?

I am going to share one last tip with you that you can make your front-end offer utterly seductive. The only answer is to offer bonuses with your front-end.

Picture you are the customer for a moment. You get two offers for the same lead generation video course with the same price; however, one comes with bonuses and the other one doesn't. Which one would you prefer?

Obviously, you'd choose the first one with bonuses, right? You can arrange them in the form of checklist, mind map, or guidebook, and the attach it to your front-end offer sales page.

Patrick Dahdal

How to Create a High Converting Profit Maximizer

Moving on to the next element in the Marketing Funnel – the Profit Maximizer. The Profit Maximizer offer happens right after the front-end offer. Hence, the Profit Maximizer relates closely to the front-end. If you recall, I've mentioned that Profit Maximizers are your main source of income. Thus, you must have a high converting Profit Maximizer that will make you earn significant revenues.

Upsell could be the core of the whole marketing funnel. Take note of every key aspect. You'll love it if you can master the skill of creating a high converting Profit Maximizer. This is the best part of the marketing funnel.

You do not have to wait for proceeds to come to you. They will come almost immediately with the implementation of Profit Maximizering in your marketing funnel.

Upselling is an immediate offer made to buyers after they've completed their purchase of your front-end offer. Of course, if they didn't buy your front-end product, neither will they buy the Profit Maximizer.

The price of a Profit Maximizer must be higher than the one of the front-end product. This is one of the criteria for a Profit Maximizer. Normally it doubles the minimum price of the front-end. I will tell you more about the criteria to create a Profit Maximizer later in this chapter.

So, what makes a Profit Maximizer be worth more than your front-end? Well, the Profit Maximizer is an upgraded version of the front-end. When you are writing your sales copy for your Profit Maximizer, do so in a way they see you are offering them an immediate solution or an in-depth course to enhance the front-end product.

Why do you need Profit Maximizers in your marketing funnel? Most businesses agree that it's because it brings instant profits to the business. In previous times, businesses relied only on front-end sales.

However, in the Marketing Funnel concept, your front-end offer will not give you, the product vendor, a single cent. You'll give 100% commissions to the affiliates that promote your front-end.

So, if you're giving a 100% commission to your affiliates, how are you going make a profit? Thanks to Profit Maximizering. Your Profit Maximizer can probably bring in 30% to 50% of the revenues. Thus, it is evident that Profit Maximizers are actually the main part of the whole revenues.

Aside from this, Profit Maximizers increase the satisfaction of your buyers. Let me ask you this: Have you ever experienced that after you've bought the first product, you find that the product works but you can't get the same product from the same vendor anymore? Serious buyers will want to buy Profit Maximizers to study and understand more about the topic.

The same phenomenon applies to your business as well, if you are offering Profit Maximizers to the subscribers, serious buyers are actually looking forward to buying more products from you. That's why your Profit Maximizers are actually beneficial for your customers too.

There's another aspect of Profit Maximizers – incompleteness. This is one in the buyers' mindset, selling versus the consumption. Marketing is all about incompleteness, but your product is all about completeness.

When they trigger the buying loop by purchasing the front-end product from you, they give you the opportunity to push them further to buy something else. When they are still in the buying mode, they're in that incomplete mode and now your Profit Maximizer offers serve as the product to make them feel complete.

This is all due to the idea of content-focused and sales-focused; the product focuses on the content, while the marketing focuses on doing the sales. The Profit Maximizer is a combination of both.

The Marketing Funnel works because we understand the buyers' mindset and created this funnel. First thing about the buyers' mindset is the incompleteness.

Moving on, it is the buying trance of buyers that contribute to the creation of the marketing funnel.

While the front-end product plays the role of triggering the loop of the buying trance, the Profit Maximizers, Down-sells, and the Back-end must be there to complete the loop. People have made the first commitment to you when they make the first purchase; what you have to do is make them go through the marketing funnel.

It's the same mindset as when you do your daily groceries shopping. You go with your own shopping list on hand. However, sometimes when the buying trance starts, you end up buying things that are not in the list. I believe everyone has experienced this.

Moreover, the impulsive behavior of people when buying something contributes too! Sometimes, they just do not intend to buy this, but at the end of the day they do it anyways. This is all because of marketing.

The concept is the same reason why shops place some goods in front of their cashier; people are attracted to the goods in front of the cashier while they line up to pay.

Upsells work the same way. While buyers are waiting to download the front-end product, you offer them the Profit Maximizers. Buyers already want to buy something, so you strike while the iron is still hot.

Mistakes of a Profit Maximizer

In spite of the massive profit that Profit Maximizers can bring to your business, some businesses make mistakes with the Profit

Maximizer, because they do not know the right way to present a Profit Maximizer, wasting big opportunities.

Mistake #1: Convert at a lower percentage

The first mistake is that they do not focus on the sales copy of their Profit Maximizer offer, causing a low converting percentage in their Profit Maximizer. Usually what they don't take as an advantage is the use of scripted video. Some only use boring and short ad copies. The conversion rate can be increased by just using scripted videos or live videos.

It's vital to give as much importance to the Profit Maximizer video as your front-end sales letter: they are equally important to get people to continue in the buying trance. The only difference between the sales copy of the front-end and the Profit Maximizer is that the Profit Maximizer video script can be shorter than the front-end sales letter.

Remember that your Profit Maximizer is an immediate offer for buyers to upgrade or boost the front-end. So, basically a Profit Maximizer related closely to the front-end. The buyers should have known and understand what the front-end is all about when they land on the Profit Maximizer sales video page. Your sales video can be just as short as 4-5 minutes, to tell them the importance of having the Profit Maximizer.

So, what you will write in your Profit Maximizer sales copy is a short powerful message that sums up the messages in your video. They hear it in the video and it gets them excited and now they have something to read about the product you've mentioned in the video.

The short video motivates them more to purchase the product. The presence of a video itself is already enough to broaden the chances of making a sale because buyers would hear your pitch while reading it and the video will make your page more *bona fide*.

Nonetheless, some of the businesses did not pay much attention to creating a high-converting sales copy.

Mistake #2: Mistreat Profit Maximizer as a lower priced add-on

The second mistake is that they mistreat the Profit Maximizer as a lower priced add-on. Let's examine the case of a lead generation course:

The Front-end product is the video course training at a price of $9.97. The Profit Maximizer is the checklist and mind map as add-ons for the front-end priced at $5.

This is a wrong example of a Profit Maximizer. The Profit Maximizer should be something that is worth twice the front-end offer. The incremental value of the Profit Maximizer in the example may increase your revenues slightly, but the value is not big enough to compete with the other competitors in the market.

You must think in terms of generating larger amounts of revenue and, eventually, increase your profit.

Criteria of Profit Maximizer

I've created a list of criteria for a Profit Maximizer. Follow the list to avoid making mistakes. The first one for a Profit Maximizer is to **set the price in the tag at least two times higher than the minimum price of the front-end**. You should be aware of this by now. The value of a Profit Maximizer is higher instead of lower.

This is crucial; you've probably noticed that that I've mentioned this several times, because your main source of income are the

Profit Maximizers. Now that you've put the price of your Profit Maximizer twice as high as your front-end, you must create a product that is worth that price.

This will be the first criterion you must think of when you are getting ideas for your Profit Maximizer. When the price is higher, people would expect a higher value from the product. So, remember to ensure the value of the Profit Maximizer is equal or higher than the price they've already paid.

Following that idea, your Profit Maximizer **must be congruent with your front-end**. For instance, if your front-end is lead generation, your Profit Maximizer must be something related, like a 'good-to-go' follow-up emails pack. The Profit Maximizer in this case is consistent, because people who own a list will definitely need to send follow-up emails to their subscribers.

The Profit Maximizer must be something logical for buyers. If you were the buyer, imagine you purchase a lead generation video training course, and then you are offered with a graphics pack. Isn't that odd? Would someone who is interested in a lead generation course be interested in making graphics?

Lastly, another criteria of Profit Maximizer is the **One-Time Offer technique.** The Profit Maximizer 1 is always a one-time offer to the buyers, meaning if they don't take it then, the offer won't happen later. This is a technique where you create the sense of urgency. It creates a feeling that if they don't seize the opportunity, they'll miss it forever.

When you are setting up your marketing funnel, you must always put yourself in the shoes of buyers. Think just like they would.

Small tip: Offer your Profit Maximizer with value-enhancing bonuses (VEB), in short. You need to understand the mindset of a buyer, the price distortion where you build up the price by adding bonuses. In addition, with the One-Time Offer technique, this additional offer becomes irresistible.

Format of Profit Maximizer

The format of Profit Maximizer is basically more or less the same as the format for front-end. Your Profit Maximizer product could be a package of a video training course and transcripts because it is an upgraded version of the front-end. In this case, your Profit Maximizer will serve as an improvement course for buyers.

Make sure that what you offer for the Profit Maximizer does enhance and complement the front-end, so that it is evident for customers if the Profit Maximizer is worth the price or not immediately.

Just like with the front-end, besides the video training course and transcripts, your Profit Maximizer can be in an e-book format as well. Creating an e-book enables you to discuss the topics that are related to your front-end more deeply. For example, for lead generation, you can offer an in-depth course that explains how Search Engine Optimization works.

Search Engine Optimization, or SEO, is something that every Internet marketer would like to learn. It's valuable, congruent with the front-end, and very popular.

A software system is another thing you could offer in a Profit Maximizer. Creating a software program take longer than the other two formats. First of all, you need a professional programmer to create the software's coding for you.

Given that it's a difficult format to produce, it's really an optional thing. You don't have to go out of your way to create a software program.

There are many other formats that you can offer as your Profit Maximizer, such as a membership site access, or you could even promote other people's products and offer it as your Profit Maximizer.

You can offer the membership site access in your Profit Maximizers 2 or 3. If you are able to maintain the membership site, you are in fact making some passive and recurring income in your bank account every month.

For your membership site, you'll have to upload contents to the site every month so as to keep the membership site running. People will expect something new to learn every month. A word of advice: send reminder follow up emails to your members about new training videos every month.

Perhaps you don't have your own product to offer as a Profit Maximizer right now. So, instead of wondering what to offer to your customers, you can head out to the marketplace and find somebody else's high-end product that could match the rest of your Profit Maximizer process.

Methods to Get Profit Maximizer

There are two ways to get your Profit Maximizer done, as with the front-end, which are: (1) Create it yourself, and (2) buy PLR products. I hope that you still remember the methods I've taught in the chapter about front-end, but let's review the method a bit.

Firstly, create the Profit Maximizer by yourself, regardless of being based on your own experience, online research, or a gathering of PLR products, and rewrite the content. You could start off by brainstorming for ideas for your Profit Maximizer, only writing down the ideas that are consistent with your front-end.

After that, draft the outline. Organize everything before you start writing, especially those practical tasks that need constant monitoring. Keep things as simple as possible, so that even a beginner can understand them. When you finish the outline, start writing the Profit Maximizer.

One thing you should notice while creating the Profit Maximizer is that the content must be more solid than one of the front-end. Clarify that the front-end course is going to give the buyers only the key concept of what the whole business should be like.

Nevertheless, if buyers want the details of it, then they must buy the upgraded version of the front-end.

This is the principal objective for you if you are going to brainstorm on what you will offer to customers as well. But, there is a drawback here with the Profit Maximizer. Some buyers could think that if your front-end product is good enough, why would they need to buy the Profit Maximizer?

If this were to happen, you should state clearly that what they buy from the front-end is totally okay, but if they're really serious about the business (expand their business empire, etc), then they should acquire a more in-depth course than the front-end.

Another way is to buy PLR products. There are plenty of PLR products available in the marketplace that you can reassembled and used as the Profit Maximizer product that you've created. There are 2 ways you can use PLR products you've bought:

- Gather information about a few PLR products and add some of your own stories into it.
- Rewrite one PLR product.

- Doing this the first way (by adding in some of your own stories), could be an advantage if you intend to build up your credibility through Profit Maximizering.

Patrick Dahdal

How to Create a Down-Sell and Save 10% More Sales

In this chapter, I am going to teach you how to create a down-sell, which is the third element in the marketing funnel. Do not underestimate the power of a down-sell because if you do it the right way, it makes a huge different in your income.

We've recently mentioned how important it is to understand your ideal customers and their mindset. When you start thinking the way they would, you can offer them exactly what they want and cherish, thus profiting more.

This is another technique that may save you another 10% more sales and increases your revenues by understanding the buyers' mindset. A down-sell increases your proceeds by giving a special promotion offer to the customers, which I will explain more in the following chapter.

So, first things first; we must understand what a down-sell is. As you already know, Profit Maximizer offers happen right after the front-end offer. Let 's review the Profit Maximizer briefly, because Profit Maximizering is entwined with down-selling.

If you still remember the last chapter, I've taught you that in your Profit Maximizer offer you always present another in-depth course to improves the front-end product. Moreover, don't forget to offer it with a bunch of bonuses. When you lead your subscribers to the down-sell page, your subscribers will see a sales page that is almost the same as your Profit Maximizer sales page.

Do you remember what to do with the sales copy of your Profit Maximizer? First, start with a 4-5 minute sales video. To create it, you'll have to write your own sales script. After that, do a short recap of the sales video, and, in the end, throw in a bunch of value-enhancing bonuses (VEB).

That is what your Profit Maximizer sales copy should be like, as well as your down-sell sales letter. The approach you are going to use is the same, so all it takes is to change the headline and remove the bonuses, and this is how your down-sell sales copy should be like. I'll tell you the reason to remove the bonuses later.

You'll ask them to wait and before they go to the next page, you want to offer them the Profit Maximizer offer without bonuses at a lower price. That's why you have to remove the bonuses. Take note of one thing here: even though this element is called a down-sell, the price should be slightly higher than the front-end anyway. But, of course, lower than the Profit Maximizer 1.

I've referred to the buyers' mindset just now in the beginning of this chapter. Here's a list of buyers' mindset on Profit Maximizer that eventually leads them to click the 'Buy' button of a down-sell instead.

- "The Profit Maximizer is not worth my money."
- "I don't need these bonuses they are offering me."

When you understand the buyers' mindset, you'll understand the concept of the whole marketing funnel. This is actually a time consuming task and it requires some investigation on your buyers' conduct, but time invested in this is worth it. This could give you a lot of leverage in comparison to other businesses, especially to know how to sell to your subscribers.

Mindset #1: "The Profit Maximizer is not worth my money."

When they are in your Profit Maximizer page, or the One-Time-Offer page, they might think that the Profit Maximizer is not worth the price. This situation can perfectly happen; even if your Profit Maximizer offer is a really great offer, some of them won't take it because of the price.

Because of this, when launching a product, most businesses stay up to keep track on the conversion of the buying rate. If the conversions are low, they'll tweak the price and the headline and keep track on what the problem in the launch is.

Slight adjustments of the price are the most common changes in a product launch, regardless of how great your product is, and it is usually a price issue that causes the low conversion rate. The majority of businesses had caught on the buyers' mindset. They'll try to adjust the price first, and then the other elements in the sales copy.

Mindset #2: "I do not need these bonuses offered."

The second scenario is that they consider the bonuses offered in the Profit Maximizer unnecessary; hence, they don't buy the Profit Maximizer. One of the reasons why you can set the price of your Profit Maximizer slightly higher is because of the bonuses you've offered to them. Nonetheless, some of them don't care about bonuses.

They may consider buying the Profit Maximizer only, but instead of getting a bunch of useless bonuses for them, they might as well choose not to buy the Profit Maximizer. They would rather go somewhere else for the same product.

Why Down-Sell Works

Now that you know what your customers think, the solution to this problem is adding the Down-sell offer in your marketing funnel. The reason why down-selling works is because it understands and fulfills the buyers' demands.

When you are down-selling, this is basically what you're saying to the customer:

If you think the Profit Maximizer is too expensive, then I'll make a special promotion just for you! But, for me to lower the price just for you, it wouldn't be fair to those who have purchased the product paying the full price. So, you will not get the bonuses in this case. And the price is lower than the one of the Profit Maximizer!

This is the whole concept of the down-selling. This is mainly why businesses down-sell. If the conversion rate of the down-sell is high, it can save you 10% or more sales.

Additionally, you are creating a sense that they are getting the same thing at a lower price in your down-sell offer. You are making a special promotion for them to purchase the Profit Maximizer at a lower price; always remember that people love special promotions. This is why down-selling actually works – it's a system that understands buyers and is ready to attend their needs.

This is only possible if you understand the buyers' mindset. Some businesses overlook this important aspect, neglecting themselves at least 10% of their money.

Criteria of Downsell

There are some aspects to consider about the Downsell offer as well, which you should take note of to avoid making mistakes.

To begin with, when you are Down-selling, remove the bonuses from the offer. As previously mentioned, be fair to the other buyers who bought the Profit Maximizer offer with the bonuses at a higher price; you must remove the bonuses in your Downsell offer in order to lower the price as well.

For example, if you are offering how to generate traffic by using SEO as a Profit Maximizer to a lead generation course, you can offer some bonuses like prepared follow-up emails, membership site, and so on. This would be the offer from front-end to the Profit Maximizer, or the One-Time Offer.

For your down-sell, you need to remove the bonuses that you offered in the Profit Maximizer sales copy, and then drop the price. Offer only the video training course on how to use Search Engine Optimization.

This is how the down-sell should be like. You can apply this marketing model to any of your products in the marketing funnel. After doing this long enough, it'll come naturally to you. The Marketing Funnel for every single product chain will look the same.

You don't have to figure out ways to modify the marketing funnel.

Now, you might think, how much can I afford to drop the price and still make profit from the down-sell offer? Of course, to make things easier, there is a certain formula for this as well, if your product is:

- **$67 =>$47**
- **$97 =>$67**

You can afford to drop $20 if the Profit Maximizer is **$67**, which then makes it **$47** for your down-sell offer. For the Profit Maximizer with **$97**, you can drop $30 and make it **$67** for your down-sell.

How To Create A 2nd And 3rd Profit Maximizer

In this module, we're going to learn how to obtain as much profit as we can from a marketing funnel, which is by including a 2nd and a 3rd Profit Maximizer into the Marketing Funnel.

This is an audacious move. Presenting too many Profit Maximizers can upset a customer. They will feel annoyed as you bring them through a seemingly endless sales loop. This is why having a 2nd and 3rd Profit Maximizer requires being careful and methodical.

A few entrepreneurs have tried it and it proved to be a great success. Now, it's becoming more and more common. Many more are attracted to this method because of its huge impact.

It's important to note that you can't improvise a 2nd and 3rd Profit Maximizer. You need organization and proper planning. If you fail, you'll lose a great deal of customers. If you succeed, you'll make a big profit out of it.

Now, in this module, we're going to explore these methods to plan a 2nd and 3rd Profit Maximizer that actually works.

What Is The 2nd & 3rd Profit Maximizer?

First of all, let's define this 2nd and 3rd Profit Maximizers.

They are precisely what their names imply. The 2nd Profit Maximizer comes directly after the 1st Profit Maximizer, while the 3rd Profit Maximizer goes directly after the 2nd Profit Maximizer. The 2nd Profit Maximizer is, of course, more valuable than the first one, and the 3rd Profit Maximizer is even more valuable than the 2nd Profit Maximizer. The price for each product increases according to the levels.

The sole purpose of having the first Profit Maximizer is for the customer to buy a higher-priced product. Having the 2nd and 3rd Profit Maximizer follows the same scheme, but taking that method a little further. The inclusion of 2nd and 3rd Profit Maximizer in the Marketing Funnel is an act of stretching it to make as much money as we can.

Applying the same concept of the original Profit Maximizer, the 2nd and 3rd Profit Maximizer should be consistent with all the products in the Marketing Funnel and most importantly, the front-end product. If these Profit Maximizer products aren't congruent, the Marketing Funnel will throw the customer off.

However, it is important to note here that what you're selling in the 2nd and 3rd Profit Maximizer are additional tools that could greatly improve the first product. They aren't, in any way, missing parts of the product itself. Don't take a necessary thing out of the main product to re-sell it later.

It is very unethical for the salesperson to sell the product with missing parts. Your credibility will be affected and, inexorably, your sales will follow.

So, what should the 2nd and 3rd Profit Maximizer be, then, if they were not missing parts from the front-end product?

To begin with, they should be congruent with the front-end product but that alone is not enough to convince someone to purchase them. You, as the vendor, should discover what the customer would need after purchasing your front-end product.

You, as the vendor, have to predict any possible problem that the customer may encounter when using your product. If your product is about creating a website, maybe your Profit Maximizer can be a set of tools or software that they can use to create the website graphics.

There are always things that the customers need after they've bought your product. Finding out about them is up to you. You have to investigate a little bit, and for this, you have to depend on your skills and knowledge as an entrepreneur.

However, that is only the basis of coming up with a Profit Maximizer. You also need to add bonuses in to be included in the Profit Maximizer. This is because you need to increase the value of your Profit Maximizer deal and it's more important to do it in the 2nd and 3rd Profit Maximizer, where your value needs to be really high.

Why Do We Need A 2nd And 3rd Profit Maximizer

Isn't one Profit Maximizer enough for a marketing funnel? How many more should there be?

Technically, one Profit Maximizer is enough if you're not after some massive revenues. It's enough to complete a Marketing Funnel if you want to *complete it for the sake of completing it*. You can still make proceeds with one Profit Maximizer, of course.

Notwithstanding this, let's not forget that entrepreneurship is about pushing your own limits and seeing how much profit you can obtain. If making more proceeds is possible, you don't have to settle for less.

Including a 2nd and 3rd Profit Maximizer has already proven to be profitable. Business people that use this method into their trade are becoming more common. There's no reason for you to shun an opportunity like this.

One of the reasons why the 2nd and 3rd Profit Maximizer work (as the first one) is because of the 'buying trance'. When a customer is buying something, they are in a 'buying trance' where it's easier for them to buy more things than they intended to. It's like when people are 'in the mood' for shopping in a shopping mall. If we have multiple Profit Maximizers, we are capitalizing on that emotion.

This 'buying trance' was also capitalized by iTunes by allowing the customers a 15-minute window to make a purchase without having to key in the password or filling out forms. You'll be surprised to know how this trance can affect someone's buying habit, really. It might seem unethical to encourage you to take advantage of the customers' defenseless emotional state. However, this buying habit has changed nowadays.

In the past, people pondered making a purchase for a long time, especially on the Internet. Today, people buy things mainly on a whim. This is due to the reliable refund policies that vendors have.

These refund policies act as a safety net and they are one of the crucial factors why customers buy things in the first place. If they're not satisfied with the product, they can simply ask for their money back. Customers know that they've got nothing to lose.

But, as a business, you have to avoid such requests as much as you can. So, you must offer them your very best.

Now, before we deviate from our subject...

Including a 2nd and 3rd Profit Maximizer is *pushing it*, to an extent. The key here is knowing when to stop. Having a 3rd Profit

Maximizer is enough. You could try and push a 4th and 5th Profit Maximizer down the way, but they probably won't buy them. Don't drag the customer into a sales labyrinth that goes on and on... It will upset them, and your credibility as a business will be compromised.

Moreover, the 2nd and 3rd Profit Maximizer are not missing parts from the original product people buy, but instead, an enhancement, an extra tool or something to help them. If you're selling a self-help product, for example, an e-book, it's not probable that a product will be enough. They will need other instruments, too. Maybe you can include an audio version of the book or a video version with slides.

So, all in all, a Profit Maximizer is more than just an add-on. It is also a helping hand. Clients will certainly appreciate that gesture.

Price And Value Of The 2nd & 3rd Profit Maximizer

The price for the 2nd and 3rd Profit Maximizers should be **lower than $200**. It's not recommendable to exceed that amount.

The vendor always has the liberty to set the price, so it's up to you. The $200 boundary is merely a principle or guideline, but 'principles' exist, overall, because they work. This price has been chosen after years of experience and experimentation. It's safer to abide by it.

The price for each Profit Maximizer should rise in each level. The Profit Maximizer that follows another one should be more expensive. So, it is advisable to increase the price accordingly, as long as you don't go over the 200-dollar streak.

After successfully raising the price, the same would be expected from its value. This is rather evident, really, but how do you increase the value? Is it by choosing a more valuable product?

Indeed, you're right, but is that enough? No.

It takes more than a single valuable product; you need to throw in some bonuses in the deal, too. The product itself cannot be sold for such a high price. You will also need some bonuses to give you client a push, so they click on the 'buy' button.

Selling a helpful product to clients will not suffice. You need all these bonuses to increase the value and the chances of closing the sale will elevate as well.

However. Increasing the value is not the only reason. You should also pay attention to the down-sell. A down-sell is where the same product is offered but with a lower price.

Now, that wouldn't be fair to all of the people who bought the Profit Maximizer at a higher price, right? So, for a down-sell, the price has to drop and the value must do so too.

You can lower the value by getting rid of the bonuses offered in the Profit Maximizer. It would be fair for the people who bought the Profit Maximizer for an original price that way and also fair to people who might be more interested in the product, but discouraged by its price.

That is the importance of bonuses. They increase the value while also providing a cushion, in case a down-sell came in handy.

Creating the Profit Maximizer Script

For a Profit Maximizer to sell, businesses can't expect to simply offer them a sales copy on the product page. There is a complex method to achieve a good Profit Maximizer offer. Nevertheless, that is a completely different scope, which is copywriting.

But first, you need to know the basics. When you have a clear understanding of the basics, you can try selling valuable deals to your clients.

To begin with, you have to establish the reason for owning the Profit Maximizer. What do these products do? How can they help?

Let's look at the definition of what these products are again because this is an important aspect. Remember, these products are not missing parts of the front-end product. They are boosters or catalysts for your customers to use the first product.

So, state the reason for owning this product transparently. What can these Profit Maximizers do for customers? At the beginning of this module, I mentioned that people would need some assistance, especially when your product is a self-help product.

That could be the reason you can use when you're selling the product. Maybe the product in the Profit Maximizer can be commercialized as something especially reserved for those who are truly serious about it.

Establish the difference between what they have and what is best.

A technique you can always count on while making a sale is the scarcity factor. The scarcity factor is an advertising technique where the product is only offered for a limited time. For example, the offer is only available for one week, and after that, the offer will cease to exist.

This creates a sense of urgency. When customers see that the deal will only be available for a limited time, and if they missed it then, they would miss it forever. Only then would they be more motivated to buy it. The scarcity factor is magical when it comes to closing down a sale.

A lot of online products use this technique because of its effectiveness. Usually, to step-up this method, the sales page features a timer so that people see when the deal will 'expire'. As time drifts away, the customer will feel compelled to make a decision at once.

With the scarcity factor, plus the 'buying trance' that are in after making a purchase, it's easier than ever to sell your products.

When you're selling something, it's extremely important to have a call-to-action in your copy. The call-to-action culminates the whole sales pitch. If you are not familiar with it, it is the part of a copy that finally persuades clients to make up their minds.

For example, you probably know these: "Get this product now!", or "Buy it now!". They appear in almost every sales copy. The whole copy should be formed to point to the call-to-action because the call-to-action is the last action to close the deal. So, it's advisable to take your time when writing a call-to-action.

The call-to-action should also be clear. Actually, it's okay to be a little extravagant (as long as it's tasteful) when designing the call-to-action button in the page. If it were enigmatic and customers missed it, then the whole copy would fail.

2nd & 3rd Profit Maximizer Idea

So, what kind of product can we sell as a 2nd and 3rd Profit Maximizer?

Businesses decide whether to increase the value of the Profit Maximizers or not. We can do this by incorporating mega bonuses in the deal, too. A recommended product to be sold as 2nd and 3rd Profit Maximizer would be a membership program, though.

A membership program is where customers pay to have access to exclusive content on the Internet. It's very much like any other membership program out there, where members have to pay either monthly or annually to have access. Membership sites are akin.

There are numerous advantages to selling a membership program. On one hand, it's a big-ticket product and it costs a lot because of its exclusiveness. This means, the access can be sold at a lofty price.

Secondly, a membership site can provide a passive, yet stable income. Given that members have to pay monthly, it means that you'll be paid every month. All you have to do is just provide the content and have it ready.

Here's a little trick: You can get the contents from a Private Label Rights product. These are 'white label' contents that you can repackage and sell as your own. You can acquire these contents, resell them to have your monthly content and sell it for a much higher price than any other medium of content.

How To Create A Big-Ticket Backend

How do we know that a Marketing Funnel is complete? Is it at the Profit Maximizer or at the down-sell? Or, after we've offered a 2nd and 3rd Profit Maximizer, is that the end? The answer is, well, yes and no.

Having 2nd and 3rd Profit Maximizer is stretching it. We can earn large proceeds from those two Profit Maximizers. And with down-sells, we've rescued a few sales that would have been lost. So, these Profit Maximizers and down-sells are elements that complete the marketing funnel. Now, can we continue beyond the last Profit Maximizer or down-sell? Definitely, we can do so with Back-end products.

What Is A Backend?

A Back-end offer is usually a high-ticket deal which is delivered to customers a few days after the purchase. It's quite similar to the Profit Maximizer concept, yet maintains some important differences.

One of the vital differences between a big-ticket Back-end offer and a Profit Maximizer is that the first one doesn't capitalize on the 'buying trance' in which customers are in when they are buying something. Instead, it depends on some distinctive elements we'll see later

A big-ticket Back-end offer has a considerably higher price than the front-end product and the Profit Maximizers. With Profit Maximizers, each level offers a higher price than the previous offer. Hence, a Back-end offer abides by the same idea, but it's not directly connected to the Marketing Funnel.

Backend offers are usually sent from three to seven days after clients have made their purchases. The offer is, naturally, sent by email. It's technically still a part of the Marketing Funnel, although it works in this way.

The Concept of the Big-Ticket Back-end Offer

A Big-Ticket Back-end offer is a very expensive product. Not many people (if anyone at all) would be so committed so as to purchase big-ticket Back-end offer on a whim.

In return for the high price of a Big-Ticket Back-end, the prospects would need serious consideration. This is why it wouldn't work as a Profit Maximizer; customers would discard it right away.

In present times, thanks to well-founded refund policies, customers hardly ever hesitate before making a purchase, knowing that they could easily get a refund in case they were unhappy with the product. So, vendors can depend on the product to speak for itself.

This is exactly why we wait three to seven days before offering the big-ticket Back-end deal to clients.

The time-span between the last Profit Maximizer and the big-ticket offer should be such that customers can assess the products they've purchased from you, the business. During this time, you have to let your product speak for itself. If they are satisfied with it, then it will ease the selling of the big-ticket Back-end offer.

Your reputation as a business is crucial. No one would invest a large sum of money on an obscure name that makes promises on the Internet. I you want them to buy your expensive product, they should have believe in your business. How are you going to prove yourself?

Some people think that you have to prove yourself as an Internet entrepreneur first. In many ways, this is true. Only established names can achieve big-ticket Back-end sales.

For someone who is new to business, it would be quite hard. Imagine you were a customer; would you willingly invest a large amount of money on a product made by someone no one knows?

This is an additional reason why you should wait a few days before offering them the big-ticket Back-end deal; you want to build some trust first. Is the trust established over those days sufficient to encourage them into buying your product? Not necessarily.

There are other things you can (and have to) do to boost the chances of making this sale, e.g., preparing an advertising copy or video, which we will explore later on in this module.

Another vital thing to consider is having the right product. Not all products can sell as a big-ticket Back-end offer. Most products simply don't have what it takes. So, what products are good enough to qualify as a big-ticket Backend?

Big-Ticket Ideas

Big-Ticket products must be very valuable for customers, and also able to make vast proceeds for you as a business. Here are some ideas of products you could sell as a big-ticket product. If you don't wish to, maybe they could inspire you.

Coaching

The first product that has proven to be a profitable big-ticket offer is coaching. This is more of a service rather than a product, but it is a high-ticket offer, nevertheless.

Coaching is when you, the coach, offer guidance to your customers in the field of your expertise. If your expertise is on startup businesses, then you have to guide them and give them pointers all along the process of starting a business.

It's a very profitable and rewarding way of making profits but you need to actually be an expert in something before you can teach someone else. The old saying, "Those who can't do, teach" does not apply in the Internet world. People want to see proofs that you've been successful before you can volunteer yourself as a coach*.

(*This point is made more concrete by the constant demand of "Pic or it didn't happen" that is commonly appreciated on the Internet these days, which basically means: An event did not happen unless there's some photographic proof. As you can see, trust in the Internet world is something that is not really easy to gain.)

As a coach, you have to be a confident speaker, too. How could you be a coach if you were not an outgoing person that is full of energy and enthusiasm? Perhaps, this program is not for everyone. Like I said, you should only venture if you're an experienced expert in your field.

Also, remember that your customers will be scattered all around the globe. They might even be on the opposite side of the planet. This isn't a problem if you are selling a product that doesn't need any interaction, other than addressing a few enquiries via email.

Coaching involves interaction. Even though today communications are easier thanks to the Internet, you need live interaction in a coaching program. Therefore, although you can communicate via

Skype or Google Hangouts, you still have to find the right time to do so.

Your customers are from different parts of the world, with different time zones, meaning you have to be prepared to follow time zones that are not your own.

The price range for a coaching program ranges between **$500** and **$5,000**. A coaching program would normally be in the 4-digit range, as it is considered as one of the most valuable things on the Internet. As you can see, with a price range like this, it's right up the alley of a big-ticket Back-end offer.

Group Coaching

Group coaching is similar to coaching. The only difference is that, as the name says, coaching is a one-to-one deal whereas group coaching is offered to several people.

So, in a group coaching engagement, you interact with more than one individual at a time. As with coaching, you need some expertise in a field before you can promote your group-coaching program. It's easier to attract clients if you have positioned yourself in the market.

Nevertheless, the price range for group coaching is lower than individual coaching, given that it's a shared service. You can still make profit, though. Its price often varies from **$200** to **$500**.

But remember, you are serving more than one person, which means the profit you make from group coaching (even though it's cheaper than individual coaching), might out-top the first one when you sum the total collected amount.

The reason for this is because in personal coaching, you give your undivided attention to just one person, which is your client. In group coaching, you interact with more than one person, so they have to share your time.

You'll find the rough edges of group coaching over time, just like with traditional coaching. Even when you are dealing with only one person from abroad, and you have to adjust to their time, imagine what it would be like to attend a group of different people from all over the world. It's no easy task to please everybody.

Licensing Program

The Coaching and Group coaching programs demand commitment and consume a lot of your time. There is an alternative to make big profit without investing too much time or energy.

A licensing program is when you sell private label rights. In other words, these are white label contents where you sell off your own content to someone else, who could use it and sell it as theirs.

The closest thing to this would be ghostwriting. Ghostwriters, as you can imagine, don't get any credit for their work. Instead, they sell off their work to someone else. The person who buys their work is the one who gets all the credit for it.

You might think this is unethical or "cheating", but let me tell you, this has been going on since the world started spinning. It's not stealing or plagiarizing, because the deal is made by mutual agreement. Stealing content is when someone uses someone else's work without their consent. That is illegal and unethical. This licensing program comes from an agreement made between the producer and the purchaser.

In this engagement, you are the creator of the content and you have to give up the credit and ownership of what you produce. You must be mentally prepared to sunder yourself from the project you created.

Because ownership and credit are given up, it is, evidently, highly priced. If that weren't the case, I wouldn't mind bringing it up at all.

The price for a licensing program, like a coaching program, usually goes from **$500** to **$5,000**.

It's a great way to increase your revenues, as it doesn't require a heavy investment like a coaching program or a group-coaching program. It's a much simpler way to earn the same as you would with a coaching or a group-coaching program. This is a great big-ticket Back-end offer if you're not trying to position your business in the market.

Promo Email for Back-end Offers

Writing about promo emails is a whole different realm. It has its own techniques, skills and principles. It would be absurd to try and squeeze that whole subject in this book without falling off tracks. Nonetheless, I'll write about the tenor of it. It's best to know more than just the basics, but for the moment being, I'll share the essentials with you.

It's very much like any other existent copywriting and promo emails, but here, we are talking about a big-ticket Back-end offer. It needs a lot of effort regarding its promotion and its contents.

As previously stated, it must be sent somewhere between **3 to 7 days** after the customer makes a purchase.

This gap is so that the customers can use the products they've bought from your business and decide whether to trust you or not with further investment. These products they've purchased from you include the Profit Maximizers, of course. It wouldn't be practical to sell a big-ticket Back-end to someone who didn't even acquire some Profit Maximizers.

Allow me to repeat myself: this gap is meant for users to evaluate the products you've sold to them. If they weren't happy with previous products they bought from you in the prior engagement, then it would be inconceivable to sell them your product.

The general tone of the email should be a "hidden bonus" for the customers. This product that you're offering as a Back-end is supposed to be only for them. This idea isn't entirely new to them. Like all the elements of the marketing funnel, this one has to be congruent with the rest, too. So, you should address them on a slightly new angle, not as if you were approaching a new customer.

Now, let's get a little bit more technical.

First of all, you need to come up with a captivating subject title. It's the first thing they'll notice. The email's subject title will decide whether they will open it or not. However, that's not the only challenge. You also have to write a subject line that is less than 50 characters.

I tell you this because, beyond the 50th character in an email subject line, they are replaced with an ellipsis. Therefore, people can't really see the full subject line, leaving your title incomplete and messy.

To write a tempting line, you need to play around with the typical cases of the characters, too. This wouldn't work if you wrote all the subject line in a small case lettering.

For example:

- o Check out this new deal
- o this is a new product from me

The examples above look unprofessional. Thus, you need to come up with something better than that.

Even if you want to capitalize every word, you have to do so moderately. You can't write the whole sentence in capital letters.

Do not write like this:

- o HEY, CHECKOUT THIS NEW DEAL
- o THIS IS A NEW PRODUCT FROM ME

Even though they might be "attention-grabbing" (they do accomplish that), they can also be annoying, as they sound like you're yelling. Most people ignore emails with subject lines like that.

If you do want to use all caps, use it sparingly and only for the appropriate words; something like:

- o   *NEW* Checkout this new deal
- o   *HOT* New product from me

As you can see, the all caps words are only used to draw the customer's attention, instead of hard selling.

The best way is to actually use title case sentences, where the first letter of each word is capitalized. For example:

- o   Checkout This New Deal
- o   New Product From Me

It is easy on the eyes and not hard selling.

Another essential aspect of promo email writing is writing the characteristics and benefits of a product. These features are best presented as a list, so they are easier to read. Some people would skip flowing text and just jump to the bullet points where it states what the product is all about.

Let's take a random product and list out its features as an example. Let's use a design software program:

This program allows you to:

- ✓ *Create multiple layers*
- ✓ *Convert files to different format*
- ✓ *Sync your work from different devices*

As you can see, it is far easier to read and write; it's simpler and more effective than talking about your product in a long, tedious paragraph.

Additionally, a very important part of your email is the link to the product page, where they can buy your product. These links must be visible and easy to find. You should place them in between paragraphs so that it's easier for them to find.

Patrick Dahdal

How To Write Buyer Follow-Up Emails

A good business person knows that a sale does not simply end when a transaction is made. Not even after all the Profit Maximizers.

In this module, we are going to discuss follow-up emails. Naturally, this is part of the marketing funnel too.

What Are Follow-Up Emails?

Follow-up emails are emails sent to customer after a purchase.

Clients normally receive a "Thank You" email after a purchase is made on behalf of the vendor. This expression of gratitude is a nice way to start a good relationship between customers and businesses. However, that's not the only reason for sending follow-up emails.

In the "Thank You" email, the business should also include its contact details or help desk, should any problem arise from using the product. This also includes all your contact details.

Now, how many emails would it be recommendable to send? The best quantity is actually **four emails** per marketing funnel. But, beware! You shouldn't send them all at once! You should send each one after a few days in between. There is a pace to marketing that you should follow if you expect to sell your products. You do not want to annoy the customers with spam.

1st Email: Thank You

The first email you should send your customers is the 'Thank You' email.

This is an expression of gratitude towards customers for purchasing your product; a token of your appreciation.

However, it should also include your contact details and refund policy for the product.

Example:

> Dear [*customer*],
>
> Thank you for purchasing [*product name*]!
> We hope you enjoy this product and we
> wish you all the best in using it.
>
> If you have any problems with it, and we
> doubt that you will, you can contact us
> at [*vendor email*]. We have a 30-day
> refund policy should you feel
> dissatisfied with our product.
>
> Good luck and thank you!
> [*vendor*]

It's best not to sell them anything here (yet), because they've just been through the Marketing Funnel and you've already sold them enough for now.

You could even send them a receipt here, as well. It's more practical to attach the receipt to the email rather than incorporating it in the body of the actual "Thank you" email.

2nd Email: Tips

For the 2nd email that you send to them, it's all about using the product. Just give them some tips and/or tricks on how to use your product(s) to the fullest.

Example:

Hey [customer],

How's the [product] coming along? Here are some tips for you:
* [tip #1]
* [tip #2]
* [tip #3]

We hope you get the best out of this product.

If you have any problems or enquiries, don't hesitate to contact us at [vendor email].

Best wishes,
[vendor]

Of course, as a business, you want your customers to be happy with your product and services. Sharing tips with them here is a great way to do that.

Your customers will surely appreciate the gesture, thus, strengthening your buyer-vendor relationship. This will pave the way for you to be a trustable and respected business to the eyes of your clients.

Also, as a vendor, you should have a more profound insight of your product and how a customer can get the best of it and take it to another level.

3rd Email: Hidden Tips

Similarly to the preceding email, share some more tips here.

For example:

> Hey [customer],
>
> How's it going? Here are some more tips for you to use [product].
>
> * [tip #4]
> * [tip #5]
> * [tip #6]
>
> We hope you get the best out of this product.
>
> Should you have any enquiries or problems, please do send us an email at [vendor email].
>
> Thank you,
> [vendor]

Here in this email, just share some tips you might have omitted or forgot in the previous email. Sell these tips as 'hidden tips' so that the customers feel appreciated.

4th Email: Unannounced Bonus

The fourth email is where you offer them the unannounced bonus, which is the big-ticket Back-end offer.

Having a big-ticket Back-end is a wonderful way to strengthen the power of the marketing funnel and reflect it on your sales. It can amass profit, as a result of being the most valuable product in the Marketing Funnel.

Anyone would feel tempted to sell this big-ticket Back-end offer immediately after completing marketing funnel. However, because this product is so valuable and equivalently expensive, you need to concede them a few days after the actual purchase. The best waiting time is somewhere between 3 and 7 days, subsequently to the sale.

Example:

Hello [customer],

Great news! I have this bonus to offer you that is exclusive to buyers who are truly serious about [*product*].

Introducing the [*Backend product*].

Now, this is only offered to people who are really serious, though. I do not offer it to anyone else. With this product, you can:

* [*feature #1*]
* [*feature #2*]
* [*feature #3*]

Get this product here: [*product page link*]

Best wishes,
[*vendor*]

In order to effectively sell a big-ticket Back-end offer requires being patient. You have to win the clients' trust. You do this by making them happy with your product first.

The previous two emails were sent precisely to accomplish that: to ensure they feel happy with the product you've sold to them and to make your reputation soar as a business.

5ᵗʰ Email Onwards: Promotional Emails

The fourth email was the last one belonging to the initial marketing funnel. From the fifth email onwards, they are considered promotional emails for other products that you might have on sales at the moment. For the moment being, you should truly realize the importance of saving the email addresses of your customers; this is done to sell future products and services.

Tack action. Make it happen.

If you want to get in touch or are interested in getting our assistance to implement these steps in your business please visit my website. Note the website you'll also get access to my gift to you which is the webinar on how to implement the first two steps in your business:

http://www.marketleaderformula.com

To your success,

Patrick Dahdal